Flowers I Should Have
Thrown Away Yesterday

Flowers I Should Have Thrown Away Yesterday

Elisa Matvejeva

OOO MAIDA VALE PUBLISHING

First published in 2018
by Maida Vale Publishing Ltd
Suite 333, 19-21 Crawford Street
Marylebone, London W1H 1PJ
United Kingdom

Cover design and typeset by Edwin Smet
Cover drawing by Balbina Bochużyńska
Illustrations Audrey Wong & Grace Yuan
Printed in England by TJ International Ltd, Padstow, Cornwall

ISBN 978-1-912477-59-3

WWW.EYEWEARPUBLISHING.COM

Veltīts mammai & tētim
And you too, Sharpie

Elisa Matvejeva is a contemporary poet and filmmaker currently residing in London, England. From her travels around the world, she has gained a unique voice and uses it to write her poems. Elisa has been writing since she could hold a pen and, with her mother's encouragement, has made sure always to keep creating. With the publication of her first book, Elisa hopes to continue making more of both beautiful words and films. In her free time, she enjoys films, wine, and cuddling small animals. She's on Instagram as elisa.matvejeva.

TABLE OF CONTENTS

time both is
and is not
in your absence
time is altered
through my loneliness
time is stale and smells of flowers
i should have thrown away yesterday
time feels like all the words
i never said but hoped i would
in my lack of courage
i feel a stitch in my side
it burns along with the heavenly light
i am tired of running
let's now rest in each other's lack
observe your decaying body
with a quiet dignity
and let time feel
exactly as it does

you dancing in the first snow
was everything i ever dreamed to see
it represented a dream world so far removed
that i couldn't help but get caught up
in my own imagined emergencies
i keep hoping that we'll go back to our old life
the one where care was a requirement
not a luxury
but that's the thing isn't it?
we're meant to move forward
we're meant to grow
we're meant to evolve
with summers passing

i can't wait for spring to come again
naïve and trusting
in the smallest gust of wind

it's your laugh ringing like a timeless chime in my ears
it's you as the smell of dust on a nostalgic afternoon
it's striking out words until you break the page
it's you leading the vanguard against my fears
it's you as the moon pulling the current of our collective lives
it's sitting still in the pollution of mankind
it's your coarse voice whispering
that you'd miss me if
i died

it's reaching out to the mirror and greeting warmth
it's you as the fog descending down on my sight
it's your handwriting that loops rings around my throat
it's glowing traffic lights at 3am
that's what it is to be yours

i want to be permanent
in your fleeting eyes
and your happenstance heart

i want to be permanent
with your transient soul
and your cursory glance

i want to be permanent
in your ephemeral thoughts
and your rapid daydreams

i want all of your running desires
and hasty loves
give me something imperishable
for i have nothing of my own

that night
you know the night i'm talking about
that night
when we were still obsessed
with the idea of another soul
loving you in return
that night we climbed down the well
in the middle of eternity's field
we counted the cobblestones
and chipped away at the moss between our teeth
that night we looked into each other's
hallowed nightmares
that night the well took us
despite our differences
despite our afflictions
despite our crooked sense
of what passion should look like
there is nothing that the well will hate
more than i hate what i've become
with my burning contents
and flayed skin
turning fresh water into human contamination
that night
we polluted the whole damn world
with our understanding of affection

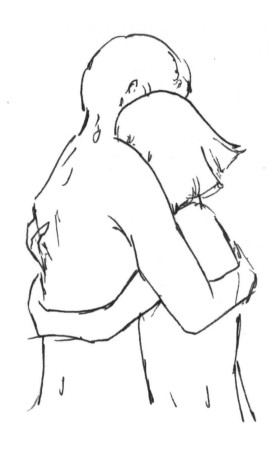

i have problems with letting go
and forgetting
the way your name sounds
when it leaves my lips
in the midnight hour
of our intimate dreams

i like the way your name tastes
like sweet
with a hint of deadbeat
and i like the way you say my name
like it's the only thing you've said
that has ever mattered to you

on the train that night
we locked eyes
and i never wanted to forget
your cold strong hands
around my throat

walking down that mountain
i was drunk that night
on cheap vodka and your attention

you couldn't keep your hands from
grazing mine
i clung to every lingering touch
like a lifebuoy
i too was afraid of drowning

i warned you i'd write about you
you just laughed
that laugh that scorches my skin
looking for outlets
from this universe

you reached for me and whispered
until my intoxicated brain clung to every sound
'i wonder what this could have been'

of course
you leave me drowning again
and nothing but dreary exhaust
is life's greatest triumph

your hands were cold
the entire time
our sweating bodies collided
in a haze of symphonic emergencies
and barely tangible intimacies
your icy fingers lay on my hips
and inhaled my being
do you feel
as betrayed as i did
when we wanted more
than these bones could carry
through all seven seasons
spring
summer
autumn
winter
past
present
future
it was always you

if you like
i'll be the sunrise
that arouses you
that stirs the great being inside
and will be in stride
with your own two steps
how peculiar this lovely menagerie
of everything we left behind
the waking grace
and the wailing space
and the terror of pungent daydreams
learn to love the smell of death
that winter brings
and move on
to pastures greener

let's dance in the rain
hold my hand in yours
until the rain soaks us
and sends chills
down our spines
shivering and melting
all in one
our bodies will meld
into the same mutated monster
one that craves our romanticised remarks
and flirty exchanges
but it pushes them away
at the slightest instance

i don't deserve you
nor do i deserve
your quiet words and shy smiles
i don't deserve the way you look at me
as if you're forever hungry
time slows in your presence
and sometimes stops altogether

i think i might just be
used to loving you
and instead of wanting anything more
i might just be
used to pining and craving
i don't even
want to be satisfied

you never thought of yourself
as deserving of a poem
let alone one about
your eyes

your eyes
hypnotise mine
like a kaleidoscope

i don't think there will ever come a day when the fire
in your eyes ceases to fascinate me

so let's keep walking

let me hold your hand
and pretend I didn't hear
what you just mumbled
under your breath

your attention
was a phantasm of sorts
not usually there when i wanted it
but always when it was required

i have trouble asking for help
because it makes me feel weak
like cracked glass
or a sheet of ice
over a springtime pond
and i haven't felt well lately
dependent on cosmic energies
and menthol clouds of smoke
your loving touches interrupted
my narcotic frenzies
and glorified self-hating tendencies
thank you

i am obsessed
with feeling this way
because it's all i've known
and because it's all that comforts me
besides the thought of drowning
in the soapy bath water
of your affection

paint me in your favourite colours
and leave me out to dry
i've lost all tint and motivation
to do so on my own

i am yours
before i am my own
i think i'm just
in need of a new vessel
so carry me to the sea
strip me of my previous coats
until you're satisfied
let's then sit on the beach
and look out into the horizon
where perhaps i'll find myself
and you'll find me too
i hope those two are the same person

you gave me life
you gave me strength
you gave me a dream
an unattainable goal
of unrequited love
and sentient thoughts
you were my universe
while i was your island
in the ocean
one you'd vacation on
with a wife and two kids
not one to stay on
to grow roots into
what kept you coming back then?
was it the pastel dawn
or the sweet liquid nostalgia
or maybe the hopeless romanticism
of journeys past their time?

i wish you'd settle here
and help us grow together

wrapped in bubblegum hobbies
i knew you
even before I knew myself
my obsession is everywhere
it howls at my harrowing attempts
to worship idols
who will never know
of my existence

i've always wanted
to transcend time
but mostly your time
and leave a mark
on your concrete soul
fill my stomach
break my ribcage
i will surrender
to this cosmic riot
and comic indulgence

this obsession
is the end of me
there is nothing worse
than blind dependency
long to be self-sufficient always
break your ties with the human world
and dance among the flowers
for this obsession will kill me
unless i kill you first

you tend to glow
like a heaven filled
lonely
pocket of mayhem
the rock and roll of my life
and my tender lies
that have been sitting between
my swollen joints

we kissed with fiery mouths
swung to each other
by cursed jazz cacophonies
lay me down
in your summered bed sheets
love like my time
both is and is not
because even in your absence
it feels like i cannot spread
my archangel wings
without your blessing

i want to spray the night skies
with paint whiter
than your golden hair
just so i can gaze up at the surrounding cosmos
and think of nothing
but your chaste head
nuzzled against my neck

you blasted our song
through the hills and valleys
of your hollow heart
i couldn't help
but tune into the music
just to share
this moment in time with you
we don't really have many moments left
we made sure of that
when we excavated our old faults
and paraded them in front of our howling peers
the wolves are chasing us now
hold me close
and let's run into the horizon
until the world ends
and so do we

my sadness begins to form
the supple face
of a suburban angel in waiting
its fingers run across
the cracked surfaces
of our smoking affection
fatigue radiates through
forgotten coves where we slept
the night my body touched yours
scorching everything in its wake
let us annihilate the darlings
that destroy our silent symphony
and sway for the gods below

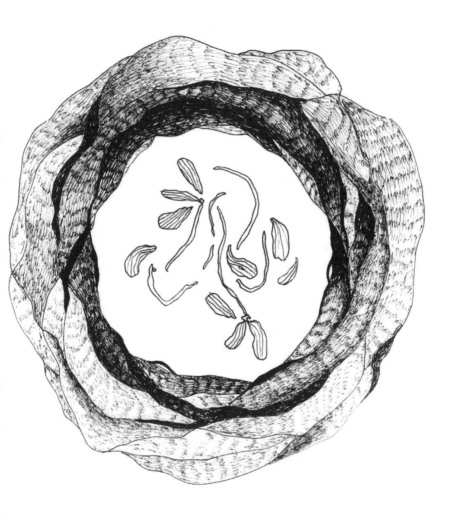

i fell asleep in your watercolour eyes
red dawn
blue marshmallows

this scorching travesty
once looked like solace
and you once looked like an angel
in the shadow
of my burning passion
dried stains of royal blood
and a flair for the dramatic
plague your distress calls
if we make homes out of people
you said you could never imagine
building a family in this one

i used to brandish knives
sharper than my mind
but never as sharp as your tongue

dry my insides with your fingers
and crunch me like your foreign delicacies
with words empty
just like the well I fell into
that night when the sky was blue
like marshmallows
and the dawn red
the whole damn sky was covered
with sickles and dimes

pain is nothing
but your concept
of a good time

being your friend
was so important to me
more important than holding you
in my bruised arms
because I love being alone
because I feel lonely
because loneliness is like
your awkward hugs
that smother and soothe me
your deafening gaze
pooling blood in my head
your whispered sentiments
in the dead of night
telling me that you'll wait for me
how fucked up is that?
i run from your love
as if it were a giant animal
it corners me and suffocates me

but
we'll be okay
that was my only answer
to your plea of love
we'll be okay
until we're not

'dashing perishables'
are what they called our
cold october days
and withering sunsets
over a city
that never really belonged to us

in the light of this sweet star
illuminating unmanned territories
and spaceflights
i witnessed these useful
sinful indulgences
loom under my skin
craving every pore
and coveting every molecule
until i dissipated
into the night
that surrounded me
like a grieving gas
incestuous in its principle
and sacred in its morals

as the sun sets
over our pristine landscapes
the grass seas and prickly mountains
this dream of weary existence
draws to a close

why was i never good enough
and why did you hesitate?
you fed this monster
our most precious memories
and it grew tenfold
within these listening walls
it's possessive
and drinks cheap rum
in the morning light
it peers over every cage
you put it in
and destroys your ethereal complexion
with its hallowed fists

put it to rest now
we will be together
once you learn that mortals
do not belong on glass pedestals
they just get cut by the edges

crumbling skyrise
coated in pastel dreams

this place of make believe
and nostalgic hedonism
is a place i call home
i made a home in you
and set it on fire
i made a home in these streets
and danced through the gutters
i made a home in myself
and cried rivers

lessons are learned
through delicate violence
and forceful separation
my comfort no longer exists
as i drift through smiles
and loveless remarks
maybe I overstayed my welcome
because nothing feels as it should
and my lover's embrace
feels like a chokehold

don't suffocate me
next time we fall in love

the lack of a future
tastes like dented tragedy
with a lacklustre veneer
of bygone illness
what plagues me is your indecisiveness
about what you want
and what you *want*
once the morning dawns
we'll forget our sorrows
in the bitter sight
of a sky i never became

in the light of heavenly pardon
your world is as wide
as your lover's arms
so let my moaning veneration
bleed onto your white sheets
let's swim in these toxic skylines
this is not love i offer you
but a shell where i once was too
and if you're wondering
the anger in my veins isn't mine —
my mother gave it to me
for safekeeping

take a left at the next fork
and climb upon that cross
for your fiery heart was never
what we wanted it to be

you sacrificed yourself for the good of me
without even really knowing
who i am

sunflowers gather at heaven's gate
they point the way up
but my head is too heavy to look
and i think i'll just go home —
save someone else

your starlit stormy eyes
were the cure to me
and my ritualistic cancers
religious wars
regulated disasters

embrace these gemini lovers
your best hope is a gamble
your mystical answers
sink me dunk me
into the icy waters
between your ribcage

tell me stories about your trek to Chernobyl
how the affluent lords
became misshapen afflictions
in your wake
the curls in your hair
inspired erotic terrors
that broke the earth and shattered foundations
of houses beyond your own social class

the easy beat made my spine sway
like a pendulum in your decadent grandfather clock
wind me up and let me go
maybe to some alien land
beyond the horizons you've shown me

you inhabit this lighthouse
upon a hill of missteps
the climb makes me sweat
beads of stuttering dejection
painful vices
drown my morals
in sparkle and shine

fill up my marrow
with everything we have demolished
and lead me into new waters
for i have spent my beat energies
on shores further than the ones i could swim for

dull explanations
with monotonous undertones
plague our interactions

i am tired
of your makeshift justifications
and your face of gold
why can't we just learn to give
like we need nothing for ourselves
if i truly cared for you
i could do so in a heartbeat
but now it's dark outside
and demons come stirring my loins
and dancing in the graveyard
that's painted inside my head

i will let them do so
until you learn to show me
your terrible intentions
and i am no longer
terrified of the thought of us
melding together into a being
that resembles your lies and my passion
but mostly our shared afflictions

my deadbeat soul
and your putrid existence
found each other
in this temple of curious depressions

you said we would be together
until something changes
i think something changed
so why are we still here
why do we sing this song
if the tune has long ended
i wish you thought of me
the way you think of her
i like us
the way we never were —
happy

i've stopped needing you

thank you
for your radio wave suffocation
your imperial invasion
your blind pervasion
thank you
for your months of organised fun
and devil's wings
in a midnight telephone booth

the last time
our paths collided
your angry fingertips
stained my porcelain hips
and your grip was tighter
than it had ever been before

what was the reasoning
behind your cold frustration
and where was the entity
my heart soared to see
left my lips bleeding
for the taste of yours
is it hard for you to imagine
not holding me anymore
is it hard for you to imagine
not seeing my eyes
crave you so much

that the earth rumbles
from my overlooked desire

thank you
for your ability to let my cracked egg yolk heart
knock on desperation's door
i'll live in adoration of you still

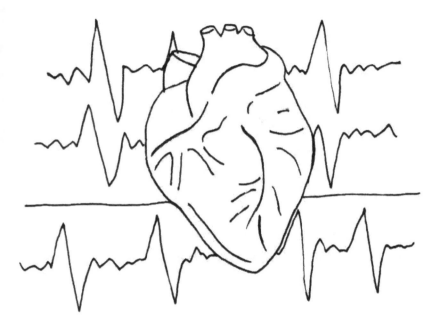

a thousand heartbeats
all beating together
save for mine
why was mine silent?
i need to be more educated
on the subjects
i'm trying to argue
like why you should remain in my life
but i shouldn't remain in yours
disastrous consequences
follow those that welcome them
with open arms
and open minds
maybe i should let my mind be free
and maybe then my heart will learn
to beat with the crowd
instead of not beating at all

he disappears every time
i close my eyes
to sleep or to die
who knows anymore
there is no difference between
the dark and the almost dark
my life and his
they are both corrupt
with nostalgic prayers
where do you go my love
when you perish
where you do wander
when my eyes shut
your lips graze a final goodbye
to my inaccurate dreams

we were everything —
no
we weren't

in agreement with your absence
something has changed –
the clacking of feet that once was a crowd
the tapping of water that once was a flood
the cracking of dawn that once
was the sun death of the universe
you are no longer
the door to my four walls
you are no longer
the blazing force to my dying fire
you are no longer
the moon to my tides
you lit my lungs
and spread love in me
all things change
someone else will do so now

i like the way
you gradually lose
your substance

drained of any useful hallmark

i like the way
you're an omniscient spectator
but somehow still part of the problem

this immutable cycle continues

i like the way
you ruined my life
because you couldn't stomach me

this no longer matters

in a twisted cloud
of cigarette smoke
my smouldering ash
of a being
a martyr of sorts
has been saying the same thing
over and over
for months now
'when did your love for me die?'

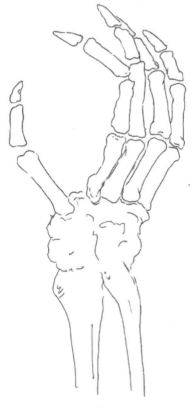

you smell like new loyalty
and old satisfaction
it's the smell of a rising tide
these portholes let me look upon
your wretched existence
do you hate me now?
or is the cynical look in your eyes
a direct correlation
to the smile on my lips?
it's the thought of you with someone else

reflections of snares
in taxidermy dreams

just let me end
this delicate thread
over our residue
pacing our basement
where our remnants sit stacked
in a white picket house
two kids and a dog
your rolling sadness has no place
in our incredible haven

you smell like new escapism
and no more like old satisfaction
our reverie was broken by raging seas
except you jumped ship
and left me paddling

i should never have had to feel
the way i felt
when your scrutinising eyes
examined my vulnerable body
while burning horizons swallowed
their suns in the distance
your hungry fingers
grazed my scars
and tickled my veins

i should never have had to feel
the way i felt
when the light died and left me alone with you
and your invasive reality
slithering across my bare bones
as if there was no room for flesh
to shield my infant head

i should never have had to feel
the way i felt
when the universe agreed
to pardon you of your sins
while in my eyes
you will always be stained
with blood that's not yours

i know it's dark
but i used to be able to feel your presence
i used to be able to sense
with every fibre of my being
what you had on your terrifying mind

what a quaint little life i lead
among these starry daylights
wishing trees
their prayers
would caress my crushed head

i'm sorry i let you go that time
pride is a tricky beast
when your fingers are dipped in honey
and shattered promises

but
ignore me
just like everyone ignores
the screams of infants

your happiness died before you did
your terror was doused
by golden-haired monsters
everything you touch turns into me

recently i've started missing you
even when you're next to me
misled piety
with the scent of lavender lust
won't you lay your shivering hands on me
and tell me where
this transformation takes us

like a bee without a stinger
or an arrow without a head
intended to kill but built to disappoint

it's okay though
i'll kill my sadness with familiar methods
i'll kill it with envy and mass distraction
for mass destruction only works
if you intend it to

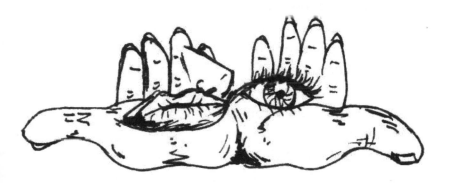

break me into pieces
and glue the good ones
back together
there is no place for worry
in my Shelleyan monster
no grief
for my picture of horrors
not the luxury
of the human condition
for those who prey on lesser gods

so i'll manage my being
and will take deep breaths
until my lungs explode
and suffocate those around me
in a thin film
of my existence

spirited horrors
of angelic frenemies
are what keep me up at night
thinking of past and present and future
about what i did to deserve this
what we did to contrive
this starry hellfire of a being
i think my love should be bigger
to match my passive aggressive tendencies
in romantic relationships
i think my life should be bigger
to match my suicidal tendencies
in regards to my being
the thought of you with someone else
causes stuttering cries
but i will go outside
and learn to treat myself
like i never treated you

i have been reduced to an abstraction
childish tendencies
and a phantasm of what once was
or maybe what never was at all

nudging at the precipice
was your scheming shadow
i know you might have meant well
but your actions
were louder than the waterfall below
it drowned out your words
and my life

save me
before i learn to save myself
teach me
the difference
between fiction and biblical mercy
soothe me
with the thought
of our forlorn goodbye

a masterpiece for the masses
was my grave
it had more flowers
than i had ever received in my life
why is that?

you would've thought
that three centuries
of tinsel monsters
would have taught you
how to run

a desolate vision
hidden between silken bed sheets
that pretended to be pure cotton
just for the sake
of blending into this wholesome noise
this deafening human existence

pour me some gasoline
and fuel my DNA
for nothing else
could bring this soft vision
to life

i would take you like a shot
and let you light my fiery heart
let you fill my stomach
and break my ribcage
from within

you always seem to transcend time
and leave a mark
on those concrete souls
dragging along
in your backyard
i asked you to mow the lawn
you wrapped me in bubblegum hobbies
and tossed me across the fence

in this sybarite sea
a sense of danger and rock and roll
of course
no amnesty for romantic treason
a letter of words that are as empty
as the spaces you put between them
of course
no rest for terrible kinship
for the radiation of sexual being
for the terabytes of mass intellect
for the completion of daily rituals
that loom over this space
possessing the eloquence of poets forgotten
in floorboards unearthed
exhumed only within reason
of silent emergencies
and innate evils

it feels like a cloud
a grey cloud over my weary head
sometimes the cloud simply hovers
others it descends
on me
and becomes dense
with every drop of liquid in the world
i start to drown in it
liquid is everywhere
it stings my eyes
until i can no longer breathe
it scratches my skin
until the marks won't fade
the cloud might lift
but it always comes back

lost suburban rhapsody
in a desolate homebound dream
this road is sadly going in circles
to encircle your sunless sanctuary
disparate hallows
of fastened bodies
rise in bygone creeks

star-crossed entities
are meant to find refuge
in the hopes of your summered arms
abandon your starry verses

heavy clouds fill my lungs
as i ride this train
into oblivion
no one waits at the other end
and that gives courage
to my disturbed spirits
i am worth
what i deserve
and i will be cautious
of these glowing indicators
even if they are just that
indicators
passive hedonism
and long winded words
that's all it is

a hint of self respect
and clear focus
will get me through
what i knew i had to do
long ago

i wrote about you
to preserve you
in my common sense
before you crossed over
to desperation
where you would dwell
in the darkness
with old obsessions
and barbie dolls
i want to preserve you
in a formaldehyde jar
in the starry consequences
of a polaroid promise

i think a thank you might be in order
the words don't want to leave
the safety of their comfort
caves in the desert
of our most recent memories
because this isn't what we expected
and your effect on me
was something
even migrating birds couldn't foresee
despite their distance
over minute details
and grand monuments
of high culture and affliction
affluent terrors swept the land clean
of any mark that might have indicated
my gratitude

i want to be
adored
craved
obsessed over
is that really so wrong
but your touch is waning
and so is my attention
to details that have already
passed us by
and maybe
just maybe
his starlit eyes
were not worth
our exquisite spectacle
but they craved me
and my soul followed

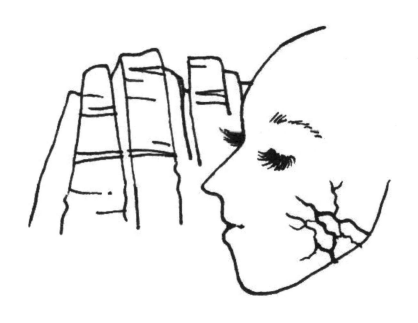

i hold on to ghosts
past their time
and i walk through deserts
past their boiling point
to forget the way
your voice
sings
when it says my name
this windy exchange
shatters
my iridescent skin
just like the last time

one day
i will rebuild and leave
these smouldering bones
to rest
to mark the place
where i built my strongholds
one day i will pick up everything
and carry my rusted skeleton
to the next valley
where the dust dances
with the hope
of a brand new day

my mother used to tell me stories
and compare life to a well
where the pit symbolised
the beginning of all
the point of origin
for both my fleeting joys
and crippling sadness
my body doesn't know
just how hurt it really is
but it doesn't matter
because the well will take all
it has created
in its glory
and downtrodden misery

i died in november
they buried my body
and spat on my grave
for i am nothing more
than a pulverised version
of my former good self

my tombstone reads:
i was never enough
never enough for my father
never enough for my work
never enough for my self

why did this ideology
not reflect my methodology
but instead create
intricate mythology?

january came
with winds of fortune
from distant lands
and even more distant planets

i was reborn
as enough

i think you would be proud of me
not just for putting my volatile thoughts
into jars too small for their wingspan
but also proud of me
because i am
indeed
still here
and climbing the precipice
even though the broad winds
beat over hills of sensibility
i have breathed the darkness
and let it occupy my cells
but there is still room
for a simple thank you
to roll off my lips
and fall back down
the way it came

Acknowledgements

With thanks to the editors at Maida Vale
Publishing / Eyewear Publishing, especially
Cate and Todd.

Maida Vale Titles Include:

Chris Moore — *Barbell Buddha*
Eric Sigler/Donald Langosy — *The Poet's Painter*
David Fox-Pitt — *Positiverosity*
Carol Susan Nathanson —*Last Performance At The Odeon*
Wesley Franz —*Apterous Dreams And Birds*
Elisa Matvejeva —*Flowers I Should Have Thrown Away Yesterday*

Maida Vale is an imprint of Eyewear Publishing Ltd,
and is proud to work with authors to develop their rich and
complex literary projects, from memoirs to self-help, poetry to
novels. Our list is growing, and has so far included artists and
poets from Miami and Boston, a famous fitness guru, and a
Brazilian scientist-poet.